I0569132

Changing Heart

By D.A. Esme

Chapbook Press

Schuler Books
2660 28th Street SE
Grand Rapids, MI 49512
(616) 942-7330
www.schulerbooks.com

Changing Heart

ISBN 13: 9781966196129

Library of Congress Control Number: 2024927159

Copyright © 2024 D. A. Esme

All rights reserved. No part of this publication may be reproduced, stored in a retrieval system, or transmitted in any form by any means—electronic, mechanical, photocopying, recording, or otherwise—except for the purpose of brief reviews, without written permission of the author.

Printed in the United States by Chapbook Press.

Special acknowledgements to my Mother, Granny, Danielle, Shadow Marie, Valerie Jean, and Jason whose love and continuous support made this collection possible.

Dedicated to Ivan. You are beloved.

"I am out with lanterns, looking for myself"

-Emily Dickinson

sometimes

it hides

in a shadow

or a silent moment

escaping again

and again unseen

it holds heavy

and makes your

heart skip beats

its like a star

shooting across

the night sky

gone in a flash

almost to fast

to wish on

body

between

worlds

interregnum

of its own

trying to

love oneself

in a place

of broken

mirrors

it was

the love

letters that

would never

be written

that broke

her heart

that left

her wanting

longing

for a love

only she

could

imagine

contradictions

everywhere

flooding fires

engulfing

a heart

that was

created

to love

confusion

did not

describe

there was

a knowing

deep within

it was

the world

that was

confused

she was born

he was born

same day

same year

same second

to the same

mother

they were

born in

a mirror

reflections

both real

both raw

both oblivious

to each others

existence

portraits

plastered

the walls

was this him

was this her

who was it

questions

left a spark

it ate slowly

and grew

eras

break glass

and i cry

beneath

an open

window

the air

whispers

will i ever

see you again

nightmares

become

conversations

just to hear

your voice

one last

time

she

fell

in love

quickly

and ran

her heart

was not

made to

stay long

my

little

bit of

time

here

has felt

like

forever

femininity

feels elusive

i see her

me struggling

to hold

my hand

chasms

cascading

who will

she be

drifting

questions

like smoke

being caught

she wonders

will the

answer

ever

come

she is

the type

of girl

most wouldnt

bring home

to meet

the parents

the type

of girl

who is

lusted after

and loved

in secret

the type

of girl

whose tights

always run

and whose

lovers never

stay long

what

is love

if you

have no

where to

share it

no one

to share

it with

what is

love

when it

is all

alone

can

it be

anything

more than

it was

no hidden

meaning

no silver lining

a revelation

an understanding

cutting through

and laying way

to all that

could of

been

what

was left

died in

pieces

each death

a change

each change

a birth

each birth

anew

beginning

this

was it

the final

chapter

no other

pages

no series

no sequel

nothing new

nothing old

nothing to be

but this

what was

the hate

in me

but myself

a depth of

self loathing

and jealousy

an insecurity

a fear of

what love

could do

my heart

in a mouth

full of rage

moving

like a

match

in gasoline

i woke up

this morning

everything

is different

my calendar

looks the same

what day is it

the battery

in the clock died

i do not know

where i am

its nice to

be home

the coffee

is bitter

my sheets

are cold

my contradictions

feel unbearable

i love being alone

i miss you

she dripped

from his

mouth

she dare

not kiss him

for the fear

she would

taste herself

she knew

she was

to much

to swallow

she

loved

him

like it

was her

last day

to love

and he

loved her

like it

was his

first

the earth

burned

the day

you were

born

and the

angels

looked

down

gleefully

on you

smiling

at the

knowing

that you

had arrived

what is it

in loving people

that makes

one brave

maybe its

the maybe

of losing them

the possibility

of a broken heart

the possibility

of loving again

after that

i want

to understand

transformation

reinvention

and possibility

how it happens

the source of it

learning to

embrace it

sharing

the little

i know

of it

she had

slept

for what

felt like

years

time had

stopped

and the air

was quiet

it was

the first time

in a long time

that she could

think clearly

on this day

she woke up

to a room

full of

morning

light

after all

of this

i come

into my own

still confused

still finding

my way

still figuring

it out

i prayed

to god

to be

made new

and was angry

for a long

time after

i did not know

what i was

asking

but i am

thankful

i asked

she was

in another

realm

she could

see it all

happening

at once

still she

could

not

stop

it

who

was i

before

and who

am i now

are they

different

did i change

who was first

which one

is her

true self

who makes her

the happiest

who breaks

my heart less

can both versions

live in the

same heart

it had

always

been there

deep within

as she

grew older

it grew

with her

and burned

bright

it was

the version

of her

that she

knew she

was born

to be

may wisdom know you

may kindness know you

may beauty know you

may grace know you

may your body know you

may your heart know you

may you know yourself

so very deeply

to be

completely

in love

and completely

heartbroken

by the world

feels impossible

and true

seeds grow

and bloom

in the strangest

places

to feel

everything

to love deeper

to be more

appreciative

more kind

more courageous

more generous

more alive

my goal is to

be a little more

human than I was

the day before

do not

shy away

from your

potential

darling

look how

marvelous

you are

look at

how beautiful

it is that

your heart

is still open

you are so brave

sweet

and kind

what an honor

it is to

love you

and most

of all

to be loved

by you

i see the

completion

like a long

distance dream

the details

are foggy

so i

stumble

fall

and fail

till i reach

my destination

i hold my

vision close

i know

it will

happen

there is

that moment

right before

you risk it all

or take the first step

that moment were

fear sits on your chest

where your whole

being is anxious

and your body

shakes a bit

it is like when

a big change happens

all your experiences

sits at a threshold

then against all odds

you move forward

adrenaline washes over you

and you are left a little different

than you were before

There are

monsters

everywhere

yet you

my dear

are an

angel

with

a sword

all

i want

to be

is a

kind

loving

and

seditious

woman

love

is in the

bolt cutters

in all the

things

that open

in all the

things that

create a path

forward

that leave

a way out

.

www.ingramcontent.com/pod-product-compliance
Lightning Source LLC
Chambersburg PA
CBHW070811120626
46557CB00002B/813